The
CRE-A-TION

A Play w/Music
For Tweens

By
Sue L. Adkins

ISBN 0-9841072-9-0
Cheudi Publishing Plano, Texas 75094

ROYALITY NOTE

The
CRE-A-TION

By Sue L. Adkins

Setting: Zoo or Nature Habitat.

Scene: *(Children at the zoo; staggered entrance, stopping to look at posters of animals)*

Teacher: (Voice only) "Okay let's Go!" (Group I enter) "Stay Together!" (Group II enters) "Keep Moving!" (Group III enters) "Let's go! Move on!" (All groups on stage)

Kid I: "Oh-h! Ooh! Look!"
Kid II: *(laughs)* "Fun née!"
Kid III: "Aw-w-w, he's so cute! Hi-ee! *(Waves)* "Look at him!" *(Pointing)*
Teacher: (Off stage) "Everybody listen up! I want,"
All: "Me! Me! Miss Turner! I can do it! Let me!"
Teacher: "Hold on! You have your assignments! Now when you hear the whistle again, come to the picnic area!"
Kid III: "Yes ma'am!"
Teacher: "Enjoy the day!"
Kid IV: "Oh-o! Look at that one!"
Kid IV: "Wow! What about him!"
Girl: "Aw-w-w, he's cute!"

Boy 1: "Cute? Uh-huh! He's 'Wild and Mean!
G-r-r-r!'"
(Kids watch monitor of animals growling, stretching, move around cages. (Can project on screen; have posters, or toy animals. Carla walks away from the exhibit and sits, thinking.)

Myra: "Hey, Carla! *(Walks over to her)*
"You tired already?" *(Cross to her)*
Carla: "No. Just thinking." *(Sighs)*
Myra: "Bout what?"
Carla: (Sighs) "Oh, you know. Where we, everybody; all of *this* came from."
Myra: "You know! We were born! Mom, Dad; remember science?"
Carls: (Shakes head) "No, not that! I'm talking about the world. How it started!"
Myra: (Confused)
"Huh?"

Carla: "Earth, Animals, People! How did it all get here?" (More kids are listening) "Do you know?"
Myra: "Uh huh."
Carla: (Waits for answer) "Well-l-l?"
Myra: "Okay, listen!" (Sings)

Song # 1:
"God At The First: He Brought Life"

Carla:
"Oh, I see, I think. (Speaks deliberate, slow)
"Nothing had a shape or form." (Video on
screen of storm; dark clouds, raging water,
and/or costumed characters enter)

Water Char II : (Slow to build up) "No
calm, or storm. Dark all over the place, A
Great Big, Cold
HU-MONG-OUG space!
No light, Zeros; Trix or Cherrios

Water Char III:
Not one Super Hero
No doll, book
Or video game.
Nothing had a name.

Myra: *(To Kids and Audience)* Hey!
Everybody, cover your eyes. And no
peeking!"

All: "Ooo-oo!"

Myra: "Uh-huh. It was *darker* than THAT!
Couldn't see a Gnat,
Cat; or Bat!
Now open your eyes.
It was *black* as chimney Soot."
Not one Owl Hoot!
Lots of space
Dark all over the place!

All: Oo-o-o-o!"

Tim :
"Wow! Sure glad we didn't have to race.
You couldn't see your hand in front of your
face!" *(All nod, agreeing)*

All: (nodding) "Yeah-h!"

Water Char.:
"Not A star
Nothing near or far
Water covered EVERYTHING.

Myra: Say: Swoosh! Swoosh-h!

All: "Swoosh! Swoosh!

Myra:"Sloosh! Sloosh-h!

All: "Sloosh! Sloosh!"

Myra: "Glub! Glub!"

All: "Glub! Glub!"

Myra: "Fa-loosh-h!"

All: "Fa-loosh-h!"

Song 2: "Water Song"

(Some exit, change into Water/Plant
costumes)

Carla: "Oh, I see I think. But how did *this* all get here?

Myra: "This world *did* begin." (Light change. Water Characters in blue/green enter) "All was dark, and God Moved over the Water!"

Song 3: "Awesome God: Moved Over the Water"

Kids:
"Dark was night! Light was day!
He made It so we All could see the way.
Evening and morning was the First Day!
We got the Seasons that way!"

Sabrina:
God called for a

All: "Firmament!"

Sabrina: "It just means space or sky!
To divide the waters, that's why!"

Song 4: "God Created"
(Water characters in motion; like-shades come together, in motion. Flower/ plant characters enter, move into place)

Water Char. I:

"Waters gurgle and bubble. Could this be trouble? Look! There! A bright rainbow appears
(Sabrina reveals rainbow colors)
Sounds of rushing water (Water sounds)
Flood your ears, (cover ears)

To wash the air
Fill lakes that flow so fair.

(Plant characters in groupings. Sun, Moon, Stars enter)

Water Char. I:
Drench and cover flowers, plants and trees. Grow rutabagas and little green peas. All join and link!

 All: (Answer as an echo) "Join and link! Join and link!"

Water Char I:
"So we can bathe and drink!"

All: Answer as an echo)
"Bathe and drink! Bathe and drink!"

Water Char I: "Don't want our feet to stink!"

All: Oof! PEE-YEW!"

Girls: "Day Two!"

Water Char: *(Waters get in place)*
"Waters in place;
Flowing rivers like graceful lace
Great pools joined and met
Uncovers land once wet
See now dry ground and space
And everything grows in place

Plant Char:
"Land for fruits, plants, and trees
All this happened on day three!"

Sun, Stars, Moon Characters:
"God made great light.
Sun, Stars, and the Moon to shine at night!
It's all just Right!
A glorious amazing sight!

Water Char - K:
That was day Four!
Then God spoke!" (Water characters move
into like-color groupings. All sing)

Song # 5
"God Spoke"
(Principle characters re-enter, visiting the
zoo)

Water Char:
"Swimming Fish in waters below, Whale,
Dolphin, and itty-bitty minnow!"

(Hear all the sounds of animals; birds, the wind and waves)

Character Duet Water/Plants:
Chirping birds
Sing their perfect song
Listen to the melodies, (Bird sounds)
So pure and strong!

Wind Character: (Wind Sounds)
"Mild and Great Humming wind
Settles, then ripples
Over ocean waves they blend.

All: "Day five, Bright and Alive!"
(Animal characters enter growling, making growling sounds)

Tim:
"God made the animals,
Every CREEPING thing
Lions, Tigers, Bees, Even Wasp that
STING!" (All make Buzzing sound)

All:
(All Clap)"OUCH!" (Kids grimace, Rub arm, leg, eye, finger)

Myra:
"After That, God created Guess Who?"

All: Man!

Myra: "You Got It!"

Song #6:
"That's Good"

(Carla, Myra exit for costume change)

Tim:
"That was His plan!
From the ground He came in God's own image (Adam enters)
Remember his name?

All: "ADAM!" (Tim nods)

Carla: "Right! Adam!"
(Tim exits)

Water Char. II:
 "God blew life into him!
Then He saw that man needed a mate."

Water Character I:
So He put him in a deep sleep, took a rib from his side, and created woman for his bride."

All: Eve!

Eve: Un-huh! That means life!
And we lived without much strife.

Adam:
The earth filled with abundant life. He was put us in charge of everything!"

(Animals, water, plants move into position)

Adam:
"And God said that's good!"

Eve: "Now Earth had color not dull and gray.
That was on the 6th day.
On Day 7 God rested.
His work was soon tested
He blessed the day and viewed a magnificent array!

Eve: "Take that day to rest too. Thank and talk to God in prayer."

Adam: "Tell and sing His praises."
Find answers in His Word, the Bible where His Truth is read and heard.

Song #7:
"In Praise: So Special"

(Myra, Tim, Carla enter as themselves)

Adam: "Honor Him. Tell and sing about His Glory.
Find answers in His Word and Story. His Truth is read and heard
You know where!

All:

"The Bible!"

Carla: "God created Heaven, Earth, and Man. I see."
Teacher:
(Whistle sound. Teacher calls) "Time for lunch!"

Myra, Stacy, Carla, Tim, & All: "Aw-w-w! Yes Ma'am! We're coming!"

Myra: "Carla! And everybody! Let's always remember?"

Carla/All: "Huh?"

Myra: "You know!"

Carla: "Oh, yeah!"

All: "Heaven! Earth! Man! Sure. We'll remember!"

Kid 2: And you know why?

Kid 3: "It's important!

All: "And we're smart!"

Myra: "Hey that was fun!" *(Whistle sound)* "We gotta go!"

All: (to audience) "Bye everybody! And remember! Bye!" *(Wave and all exit)*

END

(All re-enter singing)

**Song #7:
Refrain - "In Praise: So
Special"**

Production Notes

Scenery: Trees, bushes, greenery. Divided area animal habitat/ zoo setup.

Characters:

(Number of characters in each grouping depends on the number of children available)

Myra	Adam
Tim	Eve
Carla	Kid I
Tim	

Teacher's voice
Water Characters
Animal Characters
(Suggested Animal Characters: Cows, Sheep, Rabbits, Bears, Monkey, Kittens, Elephants, Giraffe, Kitten, Dog, Cat, Tiger, Lion, etc.)
Plants/Flowers/Tree characters (3-4 Children, can be more or less)
Sun/Moon/Stars

Fish/Water Characters I- IV (can be voice only)

Costumes:

Myra, Carla, Tim, Kids: Everyday clothes

Adam and Eve: Sweats fashioned with added leaves, plants, and bark.

Water Characters: (Suggest: Flowing cloth costumes in white, various shades of blue, green, representing colors of water)

Rainbow: Rich, bright color Streamers

Plant Characters: Suggest. Sweats with leaves, bark attached

Animal Characters: Suggest. Face and head gear; and or makeup attached tails,

Moon/Sun/Stars:

Props:

Teacher's Whistle

Scenery:
Toy/stuffed animals or Picture background drawings of animals in habitat

Sue L. Adkins

The
Creation
BIBLE PLAY
Song Book
Music and Lyrics
BY SUE L. ADKINS

Song I
HE BROUGHT LIFE
(GOD AT THE FIRST)
by Sue Adkins

Intro.
LEAD: GOD AT THE FIRST, THE FIRST; FIRST!
GOF IS!
(SHOUT) SING!

(CHORUS REPEATS)
GOD AT THE FIRST, THE FIRST, GOD IS!

LEAD:HE IS THE FIRST, THE FIRST, FIRST,
OUR GOD, (SHOUT) SING!

(CHORUS REPEATS)
HE IS THE FIRST, THE FIRST, FIRST, OUR GOD

(ALL)
 AND HE MADE
YES GOD MADE EVERYTHING

CHORUS:
GOD AT THE FIRST OF EVERTHING
BEFORE NUMBER ONE
HE WAS THERE..TO…BRING

LIFE, LIFE, LIFE, LIFE,
 LIFE, LIFE

LIFE, LIFE, LIFE, LIFE,
LIFE, LIFE
LIFE, LIFE, LIFE, LIFE,
LIFE, LIFE,
HE BROUGHT LIFE,

CHORUS:
HE BROUGHT
 LIFE, LIFE, LIFE, LIFE;
LIFE, LIFE,
LIFE, LIFE, LIFE, LIFE,
LIFE, LIFE
LIFE, LIFE, LIFE, LIFE,
LIFE, LIFE,
HE BROUGHT LIFE

VERSE:
THIS WORLD'S HIS CANVAS
AND LIFE BEGINS
BEAUTY AND WONDER
HE WAS THERE TO BRING

CHORUS:
LIFE, LIFE, LIFE, LIFE,
LIFE, LIFE
LIFE, LIFE; HE BROUGHT LIFE
HE BROUGHT
 LIFE, LIFE, LIFE, LIFE
LIFE, LIFE
HE BROUGHT LIFE

BRIDGE:
AIR, STARS, SUN, MOON, AND SKY
GRASS, FRUIT, PLANTS, BIRDS THAT FLY

EARTH, WIND, RAIN, FIRE AND MAN
ALL PART OF HIS GREAT PLAN
TO BRING LIFE, LIFE, LIFE, LIFE
LIFE, LIFE
LIFE, LIFE; HE BROUGHT LIFE

HE BROUGHT LIFE, LIFE, LIFE, LIFE, LIFE,
LIFE
HE BROUGHT LIFE
VERSE:
BEFORE A' B' C's
OR YOU AND ME
NO PEOPLE, ANIMALS
OR ANYTHING

CHORUS:
TO BRING LIFE; LIFE, LIFE, LIFE, LIFE, LIFE
LIFE, LIFE, HE BROUGHT LIFE
HE BROUGHT LIFE, LIFE, LIFE, LIFE, LIFE,
LIFE
HE BROUGHT LIFE

(LEAD)
HE BROUGHT LI-FE'

CHORUS:
LIFE, LIFE, LIFE, LIFE, LIFE, LIFE, LIFE,
LIFE, LIFE, LIFE, LIFE
LIFE, LIFE, LIFE, LIFE
LIFE, LIFE, LIFE
HE BROU-GHT LIFE

(LEAD)
HE BROUGHT LI-FE',

(CHORUS)
LIFE, LIFE, LIFE, LIFE

LIFE, LIFE,
LIFE, LIFE,
LIFE, LIFE, LIFE LIFE,
LIFE, LIFE, LIFE
LIFE, LIFE, LIFE
HE- BROUGHT- LIFE

HE BROUGHT LIFE
(REPEAT CHORUS)

CHORUS:
 HE BROUGHT LI-FE'
LIFE, LIFE, LIFE, LIFE, LIFE, LIFE
LIFE, LIFE; HE BROUGHT LIFE
HE BROU-GHT LI-FE'
LIFE, LIFE, LIFE,
LIFE, LIFE
HE BROUGHT LIFE
(REPEAT)

INTRO:
GOD AT THE FIRST, THE FIRST, FIRST, GOD IS;

HE IS THE FIRST, THE FIRST, FIRST OUR GOD
AND HE MADE, YES, GOD MADE
EVERYTHING.

SONG #2

WATER SONG
By Sue L. Adkins

(WATER SOUNDS)

BOYS:
PLUMMM....PLUMMM
PLUMMM....PLUMMM

GIRLS:
GLUB GLUB! GLUB GLUB!
GLUB GLUB! GLUB GLUB!

GIRLS:
SHLOOSH, SHLOOSH SHLOOSH SHLOOSH!
SHLOOSH SHLOOSH SHLOOSH SHLOOSH!
(REPEAT)

CHORUS:
(Water Sounds Continue)

SOLO:
THAT'S THE SOUND
SOUND THAT IT MADE
SOUND THAT IT MADE WHEN IT MOVED
(REPEAT)

All:
OOSH! SHH-SHH-SHH!
OOSH! SHH-SHH-SHH!
(REPEAT)

(WATER SOUNDS)

PLUMMM....PLUMMM
PLUMMM...PLUMMM
GLUB GLUB! GLUB GLUB!

GLUB GLUB! GLUB GLUB!

SHLOOSH SHLOOSH
SHLOOSH SHLOOSH!
SHLOOSH SHLOOSH
SHLOOSH SHLOOSH!

(REPEAT)

SOLO: (WATER SOUNDS CONTINUE)
THAT'S THE SOUND
SOUND THAT IT MADE
SOUND THAT IT MADE WHEN IT MOVED

(REPEAT)

(CONTINUE WATER SOUNDS)

(**TRIO SINGS**)

OVER, UNDER, AROUND AND THROUGH
THAT'S THE SOUND
SOUND THAT IT MADE
SOUND THAT IT MADE WHEN IT MOVED

THAT'S THE SOUND
SOUND THAT IT MADE
SOUND THAT IT MADE WHEN IT MOVED

ALL:

THUNDER CLAPPED
PAA-LOOSH! S-S-SH S-S-SH
S-S-SH!
PAA-LOOSH! S-S-SH S-S-SH
SH-S-SH!
SWOOSH! SWOOSH! SWOOSH! SWOOSH!

(WATER SOUNDS)

PLUMMM…! PLUMMM!

PLUMMM...! PLUMMM!
GLUB GLUB! GLUB GLUB!
GLUB GLUB! GLUB GLUB!
SHLOOSH, SHLOOSH,
SHL OOSH SHLOOSH!
SHLOOSH SHLOOSH! SHLOOSH SHLOOSH!

(SOLO) THE THUNDER CLAPPED: PAA-
LOOSH! LOOSH-LOOSH-LOOSH!
(SPOKEN) NOW YOU CLAP TOO!
(ALL CLAP x2):
 CLAP! CLAP!
 CLAP!CLAP!CLAP!)

(TRIO SINGS)
SPRAYIN', SPLASHIN' TWIRLIN', SWIRLIN'
OVER, UNDER, AROUND AND THOUGH

(WATER SOUNDS CONT.,)

(SOLO)
THAT'S THE SOUND
SOUND THAT IT MADE
SOUND THAT IT MADE WHEN IT MOVED

(REPEAT)

OVER, UNDER, AROUND, AND THROUGH
THAT'S THE SOUND
THAT IT MADE
SOUND THAT IT MADE
WHEN IT MOVED

CHORUS:

(WATER SOUNDS)

PLUMMM...! PlUMMM...! PLUMMM...!
PLUMMM...!

GLUB GLUB! GLUB GLUB!
GLUB GLUB! GLUB GLUB!

SHLOOSH, SHLOCSH,
SHLOOSH, SHLOCSH!
SHLOOSH, SHLOCSH
SHLOOSH, SHLOCSH!

(SOLO/WATER SOUNDS CONT.,)

THAT'S THE SOUND
SOUND THAT IT MADE
SOUND THAT IT MADE WHEN IT MOVED
(REPEAT)

(ALL FADE OUT WITH PLUMM SOUNDS TO
END)

(BOYS) PlUMM-MM-MM!

SONG #3

AWESOME GOD
(MOVER THE WATER)
By Sue L. Adkins

INTRO: (IN A ROUND)

AWESOME GOD WE
AWESOMEGOD WE
AWESOME GOD WE KNOW
MADE EVERYTHING IN THIS
MADE EVERYTHING IN THIS WORLD
MOUNTAINS, VALLEYS, WATERS, AIR AND
SKY
HUMANS CARE FOR THINGS NEAR-BY

ALL:
FUM! LA LA LA
FUM! LA LA LA

DUET:
GOD'S BEING

CHORUS:
LA LA LA
FUM! LA LA LA

DUET:
LIKE A SWEET SONG YOU SING

CHORUS:
LA LA LA
FUM! LA LA LA

ALL

MOVED OVER THE WATER
OVER THE WATER
LIKE A SWEET SONG
IT'S A SWEET SONG
A SWEET SONG YOU SING
LA LA LA
FUM! LA LA LA

Verse
SWEPT IT ALL AROUND
HEAVEN TO THE GROUND
LOUD AND RUSHING SOUND
OVER THE WATER
OVER THE WATER

Verse:
MOVING OVER THERE
SPLASHING WITHOUT CARE
FURY EVERYWHERE
OVER THE WATER
OVER THE WATER
A SWEET SONG
IT'S A SWEET SONG
A SWEET SONG YOU SING

CHORUS:
LA LA LA
FUM! LA LA LA

LEAD:
GOD'S BEING

CHORUS:
LA LA LA
FUM LA LA LA

LEAD:
LIKE A SWEET SONG YOU SING

CHORUS:
LA LA LA
FUM LA LA LA

ALL:
MOVED OVER THE WATER
OVER THE WATER
LIKE A SWEET SONG
IT'S A SWEET SONG
A SWEET SONG YOU SING

CHORUS:
LA LA LA
FUM LA LA LA
FUM LA LA LA
FUMMMM!

SONG #4
God Spoke
By Sue L. Adkins

CHORUS:
(LEAD) GOD SPOKE
(ALL)   God Spoke
TOLD THE PLANTS AND THE TREES TO GROW
(LEAD) GOD SPOKE
(ALL)   GOD SPOKE
IT WAS DONE HERE ON
EARTH BELOW
OH, THAT'S WHAT HE DID
THAT'S WHAT HE DID
THAT'S WHAT HE DID
GOD SPOKE
THAT'S WHAT HE DID
GOD SPOKE
THAT'S HOW IT IS

VERSE II:
(LEAD) GOD SPOKE
(CHORUS) God Spoke
(ALL) OCEANS, SEAS, RIVERS, LAKES AND
STREAMS
(LEAD) GOD SPOKE
(CHORUS) GOD SPOKE
(ALL) SO ALIVE
PRISTINE BEAUTY GLEAM
OH, THAT'S WHAT HE DID
I TELL YOU HE DID
GOD SPOKE
THAT'S WHAT HE DID
GOD SPOKE
THAT'S WHAT HE DID

Chorus :
IT'S ALL IN HIS HANDS
THAT'S HOW IT STANDS
GOD SPOKE
THAT'S WHAT HE DID
GOD SPOKE
AND THAT'S HOW IT IS
HE LOVES US WE KNOW
GAVE BEAUTY TO SHOW
AND GOD SPOKE
THAT'S WHAT HE DID
GOD SPOKE
THAT'S WHAT HE DID

Bridge:
CHIRPING BIRDS FILL THE SKY
WAVES RIDE THE SEA
RAINS FILL LAKES AND STREAMS
MORE THAN YOU CAN DREAM

THAT WAS DAY NUMBER FIVE
BRIGHT, NEW, ALIVE
HIS WORD'S SWEET TOUCH
GAVE US SO MUCH
GOD SPOKE
THAT'S WHAT HE DID
GOD SPOKE
THAT'S HOW IT IS

CHORUS:
GOD SPOKE
GOD SPOKE
FILLED THE EARTH WITH ALL THAT WE NEED
GOD SPOKE
GOD SPOKE
AND HE GAVE MAN THE DEED
OH, THAT'S WHAT HE DID
THAT'S WHAT HE DID
GOD SPOKE
THAT'S WHAT HE DID
GOD SPOKE

THAT'S HOW IT IS
HE LOVES US YOU KNOW
GAVE BEAUTY TO SHOW
AND GOD SPOKE
THAT'S WHAT HE DID
GOD SPOKE
THAT'S HOW IT IS

SONG #5

GOD CREATED
By Sue L. Adkins

VERSE I:
EARTH, MAN, HEAVEN
GOD CREATED
EVERYTHING THAT
GOD CREATED
ANIMALS, BIRDS AND TREES
FLOWERS, FLEAS AND
BUMBLE BEES
PUT A SMILE IN YOUR HEART,
THAT'S SMART
SING TOGETHER
NOT APART
SPREAD THE MESSAGE
LET'S START

CHORUS:
THANK HIM
THANK HIM
THANK HIM
TALK TO GOD IN PRAYER
YOU OUGHTA THANK HIM
THANK HIM
THANK HIM
THANK HIM!
REJOICE AND SING HIS PRAISE
WE GOTTA' THANK HIM THANK HIM
THANK HIM
THANK HIM
GLORIOUS, GLORIOUS
GLORIOUS NAME ON HIGH

VERSE II:
LAKES, STREAMS, RIVERS
GOD CREATED

WATERFALLS
YES GOD CREATED
CROCODILE, FROG AND GOAT
CYPRESS TREES FOR
NOAH'S BOAT
PUT A SMILE IN YOUR HEART
THAT'S SMART
SING TOGETHER
NOT APART
AND THANK HIM
THANK HIM
THANK HIM
THANK HIM
TALK TO GOD IN PRAYER
YOU GOTTA' THANK HIM
THANK HIM
THANK HIM
THANK HIM
GLORIOUS, GLORIOUS,
GLORIOUS NAME ON HIGH

VERSE: III
SNOW, CLOUDS, BEETLES
GOD CREATED
RAINBOW SIGN
OUR GOD CREATED
PORCUPINE, GOAT AND FLEAS
GIANT WAVES THE DEEP BLUE SEAS
KEEP A SMILE IN YOUR HEART,
THAT'S SMART
STAY TOGETHER
NOT APART

Chorus:
AND THANK HIM
THANK HIM
THANK HIM
TALK TO GOD IN PRAYER
WE NEED TO THANK HIM

THANK HIM, THANK HIM
THANK HIM
REJOICE AND SING HIS PRAISE
WE GOTTA THANK HIM THANK HIM
THANK HIM
GLORIOUS, GLORIOUS
GLORIOUS NAME ON
GLORIOUS, GLORIOUS
GLORIOUS NAME ON HIGH

SONG 6

"THAT'S GOOD"
by Sue L. Adkins

VERSE I:
GOT IT ALL TOGETHER
DIVIDED LAND FROM WATER
GAVE IT FORM AND ORDER
THAT'S GOOD
SO GOOD

VERSE II:
TO MAN HE GAVE DOMINION
OV'R ALL THAT'S IN THE GARDEN
ANIMALS HE NAMED THEM
HE COULD, THAT'S GOOD

Chorus:
THAT'S SO GOOD HIS WORK WE SEE
SO THANKFUL
MORE THAN WE COULD EVER DREAM
SO GRATEFUL
WE CAN ALL HAVE JOY AND LOVE
WE TELL YOU
ON THIS EARTH FROM GOD ABOVE

RIVERS, PONDS AND LAKES
HE MAKES
AND THE LAND TO ROAM
OUR HOME

GOD CREATED MAN
GAVE LIFE
WOULD NOT BE ALONG
EVE,
BONE OF HIS BONE

Chorus:
THAT'S SO GOOD HIS WORK WE SEE

SO THANKFUL
MORE THAN WE COULD EVER DREAM
SO GRATEFUL
^WE CAN ALL HAVE JOY AND LOVE
WE TELL YOU
ON THIS EARTH FROM GOD ABOVE

VERSE 3:
GOT IT ALL TOGETHER
BATHED THE DAY WITH SUNLIGHT
MADE IT ALL COME OUT RIGHT
THAT'S GOOD
SO GOOD

VERSE 4:
NOT JUST MY OPINION
INSPIRING WORDS IT'S BUILT ON
READ IT IN THE BIBLE
YOU SHOULD
THAT'S GOOD

CHORUS:
THAT'S SO GOOD HIS WORK WE SEE
SO THANKFUL
MORE THAN WE COULD EVER DREAM
SO GRATEFUL
WE CAN All HAVE JOY AND LOVE
WE TELL YOU
ON THIS EARTH FROM GOD ABOVE

BRIDGE:
RIVERS, PONDS AND LAKES
HE MAKES
AND THE LAND TO ROAM
OUR HOME
GOD CREATED MAN,
HIS PLAN
HE WOULD NOT BE ALONE
EVE, BONE OF HIS BONE

REPEAT CHORUS:

THAT'S SO GOOD HIS WORK WE SEE
SO THANKFUL
MORE THAN WE COULD EVER DREAM
SO GRATEFUL
WE CAN ALL HAVE JOY AND LOVE
WE TELL YOU
ON THIS EARTH FROM GOD ABOVE

REPEAT CHORUS:

A-A-A-A-AND
THAT'S SO GOOD HIS WORK WE SEE
SO THANKFUL
MORE THAN WE COULD EVER DREAM
SO GRATEFUL
WE CAN AL HAVE JOY AND LOVE
WE TELL YOU
ON THIS EARTH FROM GOD ABOVE
WE CAN ALL HAVE JOY AND LOVE
(SLOW) ON THIS EARTH
FROM GOD ABOVE

Song #7

IN PRAISE
BY Sue L. Adkins

VERSE I:
ON DAY SEVEN
OUR GOD RESTED
BIRDS, MOUNTAINS, HEAVENS
WOULD SOON BE TESTED
AND THEN, AGAIN
HE SPOKE AND BLESSED THE NIGHT AND
DAY
INVITES YOU IN
BRIGHT COLORFUL ARRAY

CHORUS:
IT WAS
SO-O SPECIAL
A DAY LIKE NO OTHER
SO-O SPECIAL
LOVE ONE ANOTHER
IT WAS
SO-O SPECIAL
A DAY LIKE NO OTHER
SO-O SPECIAL
LOVE ONE ANOTHER

VERSE II:
AT FIRST THERE WAS NO DAY AND NIGHT
NO STARS, MOON, OR SKY
JUST EMPTINESS AND DARKNESS
NO BAT OR BUTTERFLY

VERSE III:
BUT SOON GOD CHANGED THINGS
BROUGHT FORM AND LIGHT
PUT THINGS IN MOTION
MADE THEM COME OUT RIGHT

CHORUS:

AND IT WAS SO SPECIAL
A DAY LIKE NO OTHER
SO-O SPECIAL
LOVE ONE ANOTHER
IT WAS SO SPECIAL
DAY LIKE NO OTHER
SO SPECIAL
^LOVE ONE ANOTHER

DA DA DA DA DA DA DA
DA DA DA DA DA   DA DA

DA DA DA DA DA DA DA
DA DA DA DA DA
DA DA
DA DA DA DA DA DA DA
DA DA DA DA DA

CHORUS:

IT WAS SO SPECIAL
A DAY LIKE NO OTHER
SO SPECIAL
LOVE ONE ANOTHER
IT WAS SO~ SPECIAL
DAY LIKE NO OTHER
SO SPECIAL
^LOVE ONE ANOTHER, LOVE ONE ANOTHER,
^LOVE ONE ANOTHER

Da Da Da Da Da   Da Da
Da Da Da Da Da DAA!

The C-R-E-A-TION

Other Plays
By Sue L. Adkins

**After The Beginning/
In The Garden**
Children's Play w/music

Kwanzaa Celebration
Youth Play w/music

A Trilogy of Bible Plays
Children Play w/music

Cliff's Real Education
A Black History Play

The C-R-E-A-TION

Cheudi Publishing, P.O. Box 940572, Plano, Texas 75094